Teams *in* Education

Creating An Integrated Approach

Contents

Preface

A structured process for creating and managing teams in education is described in this book. Quality teams are being created to improve every educational process, from classroom management to facility maintenance.

The *Excellence in Education Management Quality Teams Handbook*™ was developed and extensively tested by the staff of the Galileo Quality Institute. Galileo's approach to developing quality teams fosters teamwork and partnerships. This methodology recognizes the value of people. The development of successful teams requires extensive investment and support—investment in the form of training and facilitation and support as the responsibility of management to remove the barriers to success from the team's path. Galileo's philosophy is not a fad; it is a new way to look at an old problem. These partnerships recognize the common struggle that administrators, staff, and teachers face in delivering quality services to students. Using these techniques to develop quality teams will help readers to avoid the common causes of failure that teams may experience.

A framework in which to organize and manage quality teams is provided in this book. Also provided is information on selecting the team members, developing the team's area of focus, organizing and measuring team activities, and documenting the team's results.

The Author

Jerome S. Arcaro is President of the Galileo Quality Institute. He has extensive experience in implementing total quality management in education and has developed the Institute's internationally acclaimed *Excellence in Education Management System*™, which is currently being used by education professionals to support the implementation of quality on a district-wide, school-wide, and department, classroom, and group basis.

Mr. Arcaro has conducted numerous quality-based organizational enhancement seminars for education professionals in the United States and England. The methodology developed by Mr. Arcaro is very popular with education professionals because it helps them to identify and document the added value and cost effectiveness of their services. This approach removes fear from the quality transformation process and ensures total participation in the initiative. Mr. Arcaro is currently implementing quality-based organizational enhancement programs in schools in the United States and England. He provides quality training programs for education professionals and is a frequent guest speaker at quality forums.

Chapter 1

Why Total Quality Management?

Total quality management (TQM) has become a popular phrase in business today in the United States and Britain. Even though the concept of quality management was originally developed by an American, it has taken many years for Americans to fully appreciate the commercial competitive advantage that TQM provides. Initially, TQM gained its entry into U.S. businesses through large manufacturing companies facing stiff challenges from their Japanese competitors. Japanese products had acquired international reputations for their superior quality. The quality message of TQM was viewed as the vehicle by which Japanese companies gained their major competitive advantage. In order to survive in a global economy, U.S. manufacturers had to develop comparable quality programs. TQM is the umbrella term for all the quality programs that have been implemented in U.S. business and elsewhere in the past decade.

Today, TQM is spreading to big service companies, small businesses, government, and education. The reason for the spread of TQM is simple: customers are not satisfied with the products or services provided by businesses in the public and private sectors. TQM is a structured process that enables businesses, schools, and government agencies to assess their products and services in order to improve customer satisfaction, eliminate waste, increase efficiency, and improve productivity. TQM creates better learning, working, and living environments.

TQM is not a fad. It is not a novelty that will disappear with the emergence of the next new management philosophy. TQM is a restatement of core principles and values in business, government, and society. The re-emphasis on core values enables an organization to withstand the difficult times. TQM unites an organization; it pulls together the collective resources of the organization to focus on developing creative ideas to solve today's problems. TQM is a steadying influence that brings the innate potential within every person to the surface.

Principles of Quality

The principles of quality are easy for people to understand. TQM is not complex; quality seems easy to implement, measure, and practice. However, achieving the benefits of quality is difficult and time consuming. Unfortunately, some people think that a quality environment or quality culture can be created easily. It cannot. Quality is a new way of doing business: it focuses on the customer—both the internal and external customers of a process. Meeting and exceeding customer expectations must become everyone's passion. Quality requires an investment: quality begins and ends with training; in a quality culture people become lifelong learners.

Quality forces people to take a systems view of the way they work. This is a very difficult concept for educators to accept. However, an educational system is made up of many processes; some affect the administrative team and some affect the teacher, but they all affect the student. Quality forces educators to recognize the structure of their work processes. The quality methodology of the Galileo Institute provides people with the freedom to change the way they work to improve product and service quality, to increase efficiency, and to reduce costs. This quality methodology promotes a "shared responsibility" concept among administrators, teachers, staff, students, parents, and the community.

Quality is a unifying force: it provides a unity of purpose in the district, school, or department. Quality eliminates the problems caused by lack of a clear, widely accepted and understood vision. Its unifying force helps education professionals to maximize their use of resources. A quality culture is nonthreatening; it does not place blame on the individual. Quality promotes a win–win situation for everyone. In a quality-oriented environment it is all right to fail as long as participants learn from the experience. Quality promotes teamwork in which people recognize their interdependency for success. Quality is the umbrella under which any restructuring program can fit. Its principles apply to every situation.

Dr. Deming's Fourteen Points of Quality Adapted for Education

Dr. W. Edwards Deming developed his Fourteen Points that describe what is necessary for a business to develop a quality culture. Dr. Deming linked his Fourteen Points to the survival of the business. Initially, many educators attempted to apply Dr. Deming's points to education without taking into consideration education's unique cultural, political, and legal constraints. The following is an adaptation of Dr. Deming's points for education. The quality points were developed by the Amherst School District, Amherst, New Hampshire, and they are based on the work of Galileo with Region 3 Vocational School, Lincoln, Maine, and Soundwell College, Bristol, England. Schools achieving the objectives outlined in the points have improved administrative and student outcomes. The points are called the Essence of Quality in Education.

1. Create a Constancy of Purpose

Create a constancy of purpose toward improvement of student and service quality with the aim to become competitive with world-class schools.

2. Adopt a Total Quality Philosophy

Education is viewed as one of the major reasons why America and some European countries are losing their competitive advantage. School systems must welcome the challenge to compete in a global economy. Every member of the educational system must learn new skills that support the quality revolution. People must be willing to accept the quality challenge. People must take responsibility for improving the quality of the products or services they provide their internal and external customers. Everyone must learn to operate more efficiently and productively. Everyone must subscribe to the principles of quality.

3. Reduce the Need for Testing

Reduce the need for testing and inspection on a mass basis by building quality into education services. Provide a learning environment that results in quality student performance.

4. Award School Business in New Ways

Award school business in ways that minimize the total cost to education. Think of schools as suppliers of students from one grade level to the next. Work with parents and outside agencies to improve the quality of students coming into the system.

5. Improve Quality and Productivity and Reduce Costs

Improve quality and productivity and thus reduce costs by instituting a "chart-it/check-it/change-it" process. Describe the process to be improved, identify the customer/supplier chain, identify areas for improvement, implement the changes, assess and measure the results, and document and standardize the process. Start the cycle over again to achieve an even higher standard.

6. Encourage Lifelong Learning

Quality begins and ends with training. If people are to change the way they do things, they must be provided with the tools necessary to change their work processes. Training is what provides people with the tools necessary to improve their work processes.

7. Promote Educational Leadership

It is the administrator's responsibility to provide direction. Educational managers must develop a vision and mission statement for the district, school, or department. The vision and mission must be shared and supported by the teachers, staff, students, parents, and community. Quality must be incorporated in the vision and mission statements. Finally, management must "walk the talk"; management must preach and practice quality principles.

8. Eliminate Fear

Drive fear out of the district, school, or department so that everyone works effectively for school improvement. Create an environment that encourages people to speak out freely. Adversarial relationships are outmoded and counterproductive.

9. Eliminate the Barriers to Success

Management is responsible for breaking down barriers that prevent people from succeeding in their work. Break down barriers between departments. People in teaching, special education, accounting, food services, administration, curriculum development, and research must work as a team. Develop movement strategies: move from competition with other groups to collaboration; move from a win–lose resolution to a win–win resolution. Move from isolated problem solving to shared problem solving. Move from guarding information to sharing information. Move from resisting change to welcoming change.

10. Create a Quality Culture

Involve everyone. Do not let the movement become dependent upon any one individual or group of individuals. Creating a quality culture is everyone's responsibility.

11. Engage in Process Improvement

No process is ever perfect; therefore, finding a better way—a better process—applies equally and nonjudgmentally. Finding solutions takes precedence over finding fault. Recognize people and groups that make the improvements happen.

12. Help Students Succeed

Remove the barriers that rob students, teachers, and administrators of their right to pride of workmanship. People must want to be involved and do their job well. The focus of all educational administrators must be changed from quantity to quality.

13. Ensure Commitment

Management must be committed to a quality culture. Management must be willing to support the introduction of new ways of doing things into the educational system. Management must back up goals (the ends) by providing the means to achieve the goals or risk generating resentment within the system. "Do it right the first time" is a lofty goal. Employees become frustrated if management does not understand the problems in achieving the goal or does not care enough to find out.

14. Encourage Responsibility

Put everyone in the school to work to accomplish the quality transformation. The transformation is everyone's job.

Quality Improvement Process

The graph on the next page depicts the quality improvement process developed by the Galileo Quality Institute. It provides a systematic approach to implementing quality on a district-wide, school-wide, classroom, or project basis. According to Galileo's research, the application of quality fails in most organizations. This is especially true in education. The causes of failure are numerous. However, the major reasons for failure are (1) schools and districts lack the data necessary to accurately evaluate the current process, (2) the educational professionals fail to recognize that they are implementing a process that will change the school or district's culture, (3) many education professionals are comfortable in the current environment and see no reason to change the way they work, (4) the system demands immediate results, and (5) education professionals fail to view education as a system. The implementation of quality is not a quick fix for today's education problems. Developing a quality culture in any organization is hard work; it takes time. The people must be dedicated to change; the district or school must be willing to look at different ways of doing things. The school or district must provide the people with the resources, training, and time necessary to implement quality. Quality is a new management technique that people must learn. Above all, people must not be afraid to take risks.

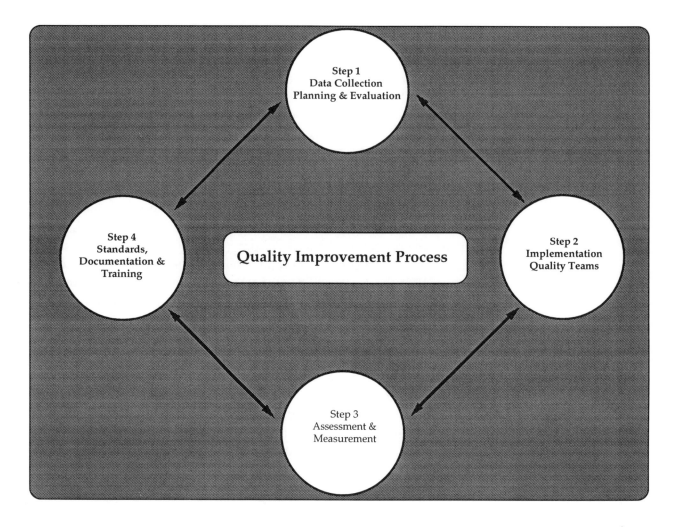

The quality improvement process is divided into four easy steps. The graph allows entry into the process at any step. It is not necessary to begin the process at Step 1. However, to effectively implement quality, all of the steps must be completed. The following is a description of the steps in the quality improvement process.

Step 1: Data Collection

Define the Current Environment

♦ What is the business of the school or district?

♦ What is the business direction of the school or district?

♦ What is the market for the school or district's products and services?

♦ What are the school or district's unique competitive advantages?

♦ What are the school or district's competitive weaknesses?

♦ What are the market strengths for the school or district's competition?

Define the Issues

♦ What does the staff expect of the management?

♦ What are the school or district's strengths and weaknesses?

♦ What are the major areas of conflict within the school or district?

♦ What future trends will cause the school or district to change the way it does business?

♦ What is the community's perception of the value of education provided by the school or district?

♦ What major external influences impact the school or district?

Establish Direction and Priorities

♦ What issues, if resolved, will have the greatest benefit for the school, district, staff, students, and community?

♦ What must the staff, school, and district do differently to succeed in the future?

♦ What systems must be developed or changed that will enable the school or district to operate more efficiently?

♦ What system(s) does the school or district use to allocate its resources?

♦ What are the desired results for each improvement project?

Step 2: Implementation—Quality Teams

Establish Focus and Direction for the Quality Improvement Teams

♦ Determine the stakeholders for each process.

♦ Determine the constraints for each improvement project.

♦ Determine the cost/benefit ratio for each improvement project.

♦ Determine the priorities for each improvement team.

♦ Determine the success criteria for each improvement team.

Support Training and Facilitation for the Improvement Teams

♦ Establish skill requirements for the improvement team(s).

♦ Establish training curriculum for the improvement team(s).

♦ Establish training schedule for the improvement team(s).

♦ Establish skill requirements for TQM facilitator(s).

♦ Establish training schedule for TQM facilitator(s).

♦ Establish success criteria for training curriculum.

Step 3: Assessment and Measurement

Assess Team Activities

♦ Did the team's activities achieve the desired results as stated in Step 1?

♦ Did the team members learn new problem-solving techniques?

♦ Did the team encounter any problem(s) during the implementation process?

♦ Did the project's constraints hinder the team efforts?

♦ Did the team clearly understand the project's constraints?

♦ Did the team have the support of management?

♦ Did the team assess its activities?

Measure Results

♦ What financial benefit did the project have for the school or district?

♦ What benefit did the project have for the staff or students?

♦ What procedures were established as a result of the team's activities?

♦ What were the project's measurements of effectiveness?

♦ What was the overall impact of the project on the school or district?

Step 4: Standards, Documentation, and Training

Determine Effectiveness of Standards

♦ Did the team(s) develop quality standards for the process?

♦ Did the team(s) develop standards which are realistic?

♦ Did the team(s) consider future trends in the development of the standards?

♦ Did the team(s) test the standards?

Determine Effectiveness of Documentation

♦ Did the team(s) document the process?

♦ Did the team(s) document the procedures for implementing the process?

♦ Did the team(s) test the documentation?

♦ Did the team(s) use the school or district's standard for developing the documentation?

♦ Did the team(s) develop documentation that is self-explanatory?

♦ Did the team(s) develop documentation that is easy to follow?

Determine Effectiveness of Training

♦ Did the team(s) develop a process for informing other staff members about the implementation of the new process?

♦ Did the team(s) develop a training handbook? (This step may not be necessary.)

♦ Did the team(s) develop a training schedule? (This step may not be necessary.)

♦ Did the team(s) designate someone to act as the training facilitator for training the staff?

Chapter 2

Getting Started

The question most frequently asked by education professionals is "How do we get started?" There are many approaches to implementing quality in education. It is important to understand that there is no universal approach to implementing quality in education. It is crucial to develop an approach that is customized for each school or district: one cannot copy another district's implementation methodology. However, there are some tasks that will ensure success. The approach we recommend is based on our experience in implementing quality programs in schools, colleges, and universities in the United States and in England.

Exercise

> **List ten things that effective teamwork can do for your school or district.**
>
> 1.
>
> 2.
>
> 3.
>
> 4.
>
> 5.
>
> 6.
>
> 7.
>
> 8.
>
> 9.
>
> 10.

What Are the Ingredients for a Successful Team?

People often ask, "What is the difference between a team and a quality team? A team is a group of individuals brought together to solve a problem. A quality team is a group of individuals who come together and adopt a common mission to solve a problem for the greater good of the school or district. All too often, individual members of a team do not agree with or support the team's activities. Members of a quality team recognize that the greater good of the school or district is the driving force and they are unified in supporting all of the team's activities. Quality team members may not fully agree with the team's action, but they always support the team's actions.

The following are key elements of a quality team:

♦ **Commitment:** Administrators, supervisors, and staff support the team's mission

♦ **Mission:** Team members understand what they are expected to achieve

♦ **Objectives:** Team members work on tasks that are consistent with the mission

♦ **Trust:** Team members trust and respect each other and are willing to invest in one another

♦ **Meetings:** Team meetings are efficient and produce results

♦ **Shared responsibility:** Team members recognize the interdependency for success that exists within the team

♦ **Conflict:** Conflict is anticipated and eliminated before it becomes divisive

♦ **Roles and responsibilities:** Team members know what is expected of them

♦ **Participation:** Everyone on the team participates in all activities

♦ **Communication:** Information is shared with all members and team activities are communicated to all staff

The Team Assessment Matrix illustrated below is used as an evaluation tool by quality teams to periodically assess their effectiveness. Once completed, the Team Assessment Matrix can help to identify the team's strengths and weaknesses, determine what could have been done to improve the effectiveness of the team, and establish whether or not the team was successful.

Team Assessment Matrix

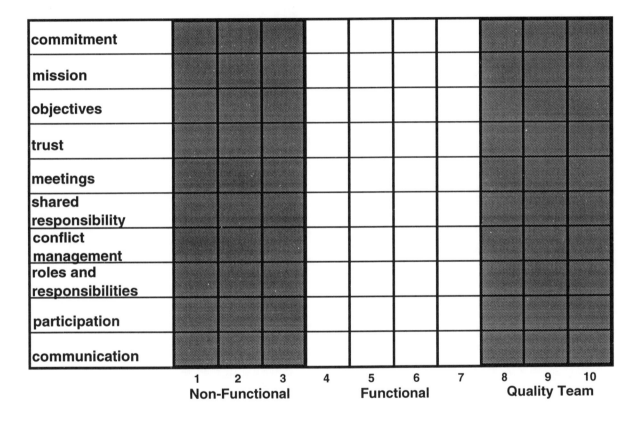

	1	2	3	4	5	6	7	8	9	10
	Non-Functional				**Functional**			**Quality Team**		

Chapter 3

Stages of Successful Team Building

In the previous chapter, team effectiveness was evaluated. In this chapter, the process used to develop quality teams is discussed. Two types of quality teams are described in this book: the quality steering committee and quality task teams. A quality steering committee provides guidance, support, and direction for quality task teams. A quality steering committee is an ongoing committee. Quality task teams focus on solving specific problems and are organized for a specific task and for a specific period of time.

One of the major reasons teams fail is the lack of organizational-wide focus. The quality steering committee provides quality task teams with an organizational-wide focus. The first section of this chapter focuses on the creation of the quality steering committee. The process schools use to develop quality team programs is reviewed in detail.

Commitment

The first ingredient necessary for a successful program is commitment. There must be commitment from management for the program. If the program does not have management's full support, it will fail. The school board, superintendent of schools, and the district or school's management team must be committed to the program. Quality programs force change into the environment. The culture of the school or district is changed. A quality culture requires people to look at doing things differently. Change creates fear in an organization. It is management's commitment that removes the fear from the organization and encourages people to do things differently.

Management commitment also eliminates the fear of failure. In a quality culture it is safe to take risks. We have a saying at the Galileo Quality Institute that it is okay to fail forward. Failing is viewed as a learning tool which is an inherent characteristic of continuous improvement. It is easier for people to become risk takers if they know that management will support them in their efforts even if their efforts result in failure. The only time failure is unacceptable is when people fail to learn from the experience. For example, when we were working with the quality coordinator for a government agency in England on a project to move quality into the county's schools, the quality coordinator's manager stated that it was okay to fail within the family, but that he would hand the quality coordinator his head if he failed outside the family. The net effect of this statement was that it paralyzed the individual. The quality coordinator was afraid to make any decisions or recommendations. The program became ineffective.

Avoid the program stigma. At one time or another many people have asked, "Is this the program of the month?" All too often, schools implement a quality program just for the sake of claiming to be a quality school. For example, the superintendent of a district in Connecticut that was implementing a quality program called our office to ask for help in developing a training program for his quality teams. The superintendent stated that there were fourteen schools in his district and that each school elected representatives to quality improvement teams. The district had limited funds but needed to purchase a training program. The superintendent stated that he "had to train the teams before he turned them loose." When asked what the teams were going to work on, who was going to coordinate the activities of the teams, and for what purpose the teams were created, he could not answer. The superintendent wanted the people trained so that he could get on with his next task. He was not committed to the success of the program. This is not an example of a quality program. This is an example of quality circles, which were unsuccessful in the past.

When we were conducting a quality workshop in Bristol, England, the quality coordinator for a college from Birmingham, England, stated that, "We have 48 quality improvement teams in our college." This individual was extremely proud of the fact that he managed 48 quality teams. When asked what the teams were doing, he could not say. In fact, he stated, "I don't know what each team is doing but we have 48 teams." The number of teams was more important to this individual than the outcomes the teams achieved. Approximately six months later, the individual was contacted to see how his quality program was going. He said that it was no longer in existence because the people had lost interest in the program. That outcome could have been prevented had the individual been careful to demonstrate desired results to the staff so that they would take the program seriously.

Quality Steering Committee

In the preceding example in which the superintendent wanted to find a training program for his quality team, he did not anticipate or plan for the establishment of a district-wide quality steering committee. We outlined the risks that he was taking by not providing the teams with direction and support and provided him with data that showed that the primary reason quality teams fail is that they do not receive the support and direction from the administrative team that is necessary for them to complete their task. We also reminded him of our original resistance to establishing quality steering committees because they got in the way of getting the job done. However, our experience in implementing quality programs in education clearly shows that a program will not be successful unless the district or school establishes a quality steering committee. In this instance, the superintendent insisted that the district would not establish a district-wide quality steering committee. Because we would not change our proposal, the district selected another organization to provide training for the teams that supported his position relative to the establishment of a quality steering committee.

All of the stakeholders of education are ultimately represented on the quality steering committee. Initially, the steering committee may be comprised of members of the school board, teaching staff, administrators, and support staff. As the program expands, the composition of the committee should be expanded to include government representatives, business and community leaders, parents, and students. The steering committee helps to establish an alliance between education, business, and government. It promotes greater participation in the education process by students and parents. The committee provides direction and resources for the quality teams. Above all, the committee prevents an individual or group of individuals from sabotaging the program.

As previously stated, quality is change. It forces people to do things in a different way. Unfortunately, some people cannot change and some people do not want to change. These people will do everything in their power to destroy such a program. The steering committee prevents these people from getting their way. In one district in northern Maine, the director for the school became ill and was absent from the school for approximately six weeks. During that period of time one of the instructors threatened the other TQM facilitators in the program and did everything in his power to prevent the program from going forward. The behavior of this individual was brought to the attention of the steering committee. The steering committee supported the majority of the staff in their efforts to develop a quality school. Once the individual found out that he did not have a platform from which to promote his cause, he blended into the program. Has this individual adopted a quality philosophy? Probably not. Based on our experience, however, a program will not succeed unless there is either a school-wide or district-wide steering committee in place.

Problem Definition

Before a quality team is established, the problem that the team is expected to solve must be defined. All too often, the reverse happens. The team is selected and then asked to find a problem to solve. The problem the team is working on should determine the skill requirements for the team members. It will determine the stakeholders of the process and will direct the team formation process. The problem definition must be very specific. A very broad problem statement, such as solve the communication problem, leads to chaos and wasted effort.

It is strongly recommended that the problem be defined in very narrow limits and that a definite time line for the team be established. This will allow for the identification of the constraints under which the team will operate and the life cycle for the team. The team should not be left with open-ended items to decide themselves.

For example, the media commonly report that students are achieving poor grades in science. One school established a quality team to develop a process that will result in a 10% improvement in science grades for all students. The team had six months in which to complete its task. This is an admirable goal, one with which few could argue. However, where does the team begin? How will the team's success be measured? Improving science grades encompasses numerous tasks. Homework skills, teacher delivery skills, student retention skills, student application skills, and many others need to be improved before the overall objective can be reached. I asked the team to narrow its focus, and the team disagreed. They said they wanted to achieve this objective. I then asked the team to list all of the things that a student did that contributed to his or her ability to learn math. The list become so long that the team realized it could not be successful unless it narrowed its focus. As a result of this exercise, the team decided that it wanted to help students improve homework skills.

It cannot be stressed enough: **the problem must be clearly defined, and it must have a very narrow focus**. Attention to detail in these two areas will help to ensure the success of the team. It will minimize the conflict that can develop between the team and the education system and ensure that everyone on the team is working on the same problem. A little effort in these areas will provide substantial rewards later on.

Chapter 4

Quality Task Teams

In the previous chapter, the process to develop a quality team focus in a school or district was reviewed. This chapter focuses on what a school or district must do to develop quality teams. Quality task teams (also known as improvement teams) utilize resources more effectively, increase organizational effectiveness, increase the quality of educational programs, and create better learning and working environments.

The following matrix can be used to assess past associations with teams. How did the teams rate? What ingredients were missing from the teams? Could the teams have been more effective if all of the ingredients were present?

Team Organization Assessment Matrix

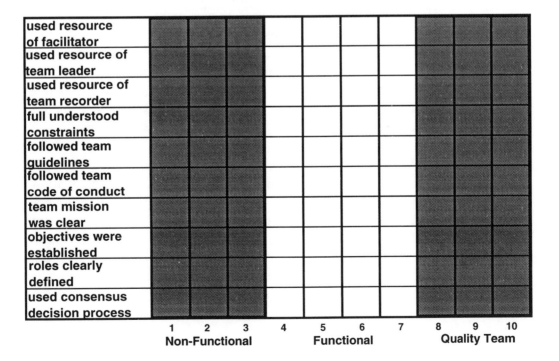

	1	2	3	4	5	6	7	8	9	10
used resource of facilitator	▓	▓	▓					▓	▓	▓
used resource of team leader	▓	▓	▓					▓	▓	▓
used resource of team recorder	▓	▓	▓					▓	▓	▓
full understood constraints	▓	▓	▓					▓	▓	▓
followed team guidelines	▓	▓	▓					▓	▓	▓
followed team code of conduct	▓	▓	▓					▓	▓	▓
team mission was clear	▓	▓	▓					▓	▓	▓
objectives were established	▓	▓	▓					▓	▓	▓
roles clearly defined	▓	▓	▓					▓	▓	▓
used consensus decision process	▓	▓	▓					▓	▓	▓
	Non-Functional				**Functional**			**Quality Team**		

The Team Organization Assessment Matrix is a tool teams use to identify how they can become more effective. The goal is to rate every category a 10 for every team. Continuous improvement also applies to team activities. This tool helps teams to identify specific areas for improvement in a nonthreatening and nonjudgmental manner.

Team Constraints

Before beginning any work, quality teams must be told what constraints govern the task. The team should not be allowed to begin work until all the issues affecting their effort are clearly understood. Constraints are bounds. They limit what the team can do. Generally, constraints can be classified as economic, political, cultural, structural, personal, or geographic. A major cause of failure for quality teams is that the team is not made aware of the constraints that limit their activities prior to initiating the task.

By illustration, at a workshop we conducted in Bristol, England, another participant asked if we could help him to understand why his school's refectory (lunchroom) quality team failed. The gentleman explained that the school had established a quality team to restructure the services provided by the refectory to the students and staff. He further explained that the team was extremely diligent in efforts: they met on a regular basis, collected data from the staff and students, examined other school and college refectory operations, and developed a solution that every member of the team could support. However, when the solution was presented to management, it was rejected. The team was demoralized, and the school had difficulty in creating other teams. The gentleman asked where they went wrong.

We asked him why the management team rejected the team's recommendation. He explained that the team's recommendation included spending money to renovate the refectory and building an addition to the refectory area to provide more space. He explained that the school did not have the money to implement the recommendations of the refectory quality team. I asked him if the team had been aware of the financial constraints. He said that they were not specifically told that they could not spend any money, but that everyone in the school knew that the school did not have any money. We asked how everyone knew that the school was short of funds, and he said that it was common knowledge. We also asked if the school would have implemented the team's recommendations if they had the necessary funds. He explained that the management team liked the solution, and the funding was the only problem.

In this example, no one ever told the refectory quality team specifically that they could not spend any money. The constraints were not clearly identified and stated for the team. The refectory quality team spent six months collecting data, surveying customers, and benchmarking their refectory against other refectory services managed by other schools in the area. When I contacted the team members, every one of them said that they would have developed an alternative solution had they known of the financial constraints.

Teams must know what they can and cannot do. If constraints are not clearly identified for the team prior to initiating any work, there is a good chance that the team will fail and that the team members will become frustrated in their efforts. In sports, every team member knows the rules before the game starts. Everyone understands what is expected of him or her. Quality teams are just like sports teams. They must know the rules before they start the improvement process. Quality teams must know what is expected of them.

Team Concept

Who should participate in a quality team? The question seems simple enough. However, the answer will determine the success or failure of the team. What is the difference between a group and a team? All too often, people assemble into a group and expect to function as a team. According to our definition, a group is an assembly of people who are called together to work on a specific task or project. The members of the group may know each other and may work together. They may even be friends and socialize together. These, however, are not characteristics of a successful team. When push comes to shove, the members tend to act in their own best interests.

A team shares a common vision and purpose. Personal friendship is not a prerequisite to joining the team. Every team member supports and believes in the vision adopted by the group. The vision may also be created for the group by management. The vision can be small or it can be large. What is important is that the team members support the vision. The vision must unite the group into a cohesive team. Everyone must work together to attain a common objective. Every member of the team recognizes his or her responsibility to the other team members.

We have adopted a policy at the Galileo Quality Institute that helps the staff to keep abreast of recent developments in the science of quality management. Each month each staff member is required to read a book of his or her choice on the subject of quality management. At the end of the month each person writes a one- or two-page summary of the book he or she read. All of the summaries are distributed to everyone in the Institute. This expands our ability to read new material and helps individual staff members to focus on those topics of most personal interest. I explained this process at a workshop I was conducting in England. One of the participants asked, "What happens when someone doesn't read a book?" I told him that has never happened. If a team member should fail to read a book, the person knows that he or she has let the rest of the team down. The team doesn't have to force the member to read the book: each member recognizes his or her responsibility to the other team members.

The refectory team example drove home the message of a team to the group. The members of the group began to examine their own motives for joining the team. One member of the group said that he now realized why they had failed to work together as a team. The group was comprised of very bright and intelligent individuals who each possessed expertise in a specific area of education. They were very good at what they did. However, they never had to work together as a team. The environment had changed, and the only way the group could exist in the future was for the group to become a team.

Team Formation

There are several methods that can be used to form a quality team. One method we use is the **stakeholder process**. In the stakeholder process all of the people or organizations who are customers of or suppliers to the process under review are identified. For example, a large school system attempted to reduce its transportation budget by reducing the number of bus stops and bus routes. Someone suggested that the school board adopt a transportation plan that asked the students to get their bus at the school nearest their house. It was a minor inconvenience for the students, but it had the potential to save the city over $250,000 per year. The transportation committee evaluated the plan and stated, "It is a sound proposal that provides the city with significant cost savings." The plan was scheduled to go into effect on the Monday following a vacation week.

At a school board meeting prior to the implementation of the plan, a parent asked the board who was going to be responsible for the safety of the children while they waited for the buses at the schools. The parent explained that there would be many unsupervised students at each school waiting to get the bus. The parent suggested that the collection of all of the students in a central area would create problems of safety that the transportation committee had not considered. The school board reevaluated the proposal and discovered that the parent was correct in this assumption. In addition, the city's insurance carrier requires supervision of students when they are on school grounds for authorized activities. The proposal was not implemented because the cost to do so was greater than the proposed cost savings.

This situation could have been avoided if the transportation committee evaluating the proposal had included representatives from all of the stakeholders of the transportation process, i.e., students, parents, transportation officials, administrators, teachers, and custodial staff. In fact, one of the custodial staff commented in the local paper that the plan would not work because no one would be available to watch the students while they were waiting for the bus. The reporter asked him why he didn't express his concerns at one of the meetings. He said that no one ever asked him.

Team Selection

Membership in a quality team is usually voluntary. However, members can be appointed to serve on task teams. They can be appointed to serve on the team because of their position of employment; board policy may dictate representation on the team. The members selected to serve on the team must have an interest in solving the problem, or their field of expertise may necessitate their participation in task teams. However selected, task team members cannot be uninterested individuals who are forced to serve on a team. They must want to help solve the problem. If they have no interest in solving the problem, they will not contribute to the activities of the team and, more importantly, they will not support the team's recommendation. This makes it extremely difficult for the team to gain broad support for their solution.

Again, the team is comprised of representatives from the stakeholders in the process. In England at a college we are working with, a refectory team was established to develop recommendations to improve the quality of the food and service provided by the refectory to the staff and students. The team is comprised of a representative from the senior management team, the refectory staff, the support staff, the teaching staff, the student body, the health and safety officer, and an external facilitator. Some of the members were appointed to the team, and some were elected to serve on the team. This is an excellent example of a cross-functional team comprised of the stakeholders of the process being reviewed. The voice of the customer is reflected in the team's activities.

Team Organization

The following guidelines are suggested for the organization of a quality team.

Facilitator

Many education professionals say that they do not need a facilitator to manage their team meetings. They are professionals who know how to research and solve problems. Unfortunately, most people join a team with certain biases. Subconsciously, some try to manage and direct the process. This subconscious power struggle for dominance can sabotage the team process. A TQM facilitator is someone who has an objective view of the problem. It is the facilitator's job to keep the team focused on the task at hand. The facilitator should possess good people skills and should have a detailed understanding of the use and application of TQM tools and techniques. All too often, teams struggle through issues that could easily be resolved if a facilitator were managing the team meetings. The facilitator must understand TQM. This cannot be an on-the-job learning experience; if it is, the team will fail.

Team Leader

The team leader should be selected by the group. The team leader should be selected at the initial team meeting. The facilitator should manage the process for selecting the team leader. Usually, the team members vote on the team leader. The common situation in which the most popular person in the group becomes the team leader must be avoided. This individual many not be the best person to direct the team. A team leader should have good leadership skills and experience working with groups. He or she should also have experience in the use of quality tools and techniques. The team leader has something to gain by seeking an objective solution to fix the problem.

Team Recorder

The comment most frequently heard from schools is that the quality team did an excellent job solving the problem, but that they did not have time to document what they did. A major function of a quality team is to develop an experience base that can be shared with other members of the school or district. Therefore, every team should select someone to be the team recorder. It is the responsibility of the team recorder to keep minutes of the meetings, to publish an agenda for all meetings, and to document how the team solved the problem, the tools that were used, the problems encountered, and the benefits derived for the district, school, student, staff, or community.

Code of Conduct

Quality schools establish a code of conduct to govern team activities. A code of conduct eliminates many of the root causes of team conflict and clearly establishes expectations for team members. The following is an example of a code of conduct established by a quality school. It can be modified for another school or district.

- ◆ Teams will value the rights of individual members.

- ◆ Teams will critique the idea, not the person.

- ◆ Teams will allow every member to fully express his or her ideas.

- ◆ Teams will immediately resolve areas of conflict.

- ◆ Teams will utilize the group consensus decision-making model to reach all decisions.

- ◆ Teams members will be attentive during team meetings.

- ◆ Team members will not be distracted from team business during team meetings.

- ◆ Team members will complete all tasks assigned to them.

- ◆ Team members will publicly support the team's decisions and activities.

- ◆ Team members will attend team meetings

The code of conduct is a simple tool that quality schools use to govern the way teams operate. Generally, the code of conduct is established by the school-wide or district-wide quality steering committee. If the steering committee has not established a code of conduct, the quality task teams should make it a priority task.

Chapter 5

Managing Team Meetings

As discussed in the previous chapter, every team should have ground rules to govern the team's activities and meetings. One of the major causes of failure in implementing quality is the inability of people in a team to build trust among themselves. Quality teams should also build partnerships with all the stakeholders of the process. As the level of trust increases among the team members and between the team and the stakeholders, the team will create better learning and working environments. The following are hints for managing successful team meetings.

Code of Conduct

One of the first organizational items the team should discuss is the code of conduct. Individual members should agree to abide by the code of conduct. Members who cannot abide by the code of conduct should be excused from the team.

Meeting Location

Schedule a convenient meeting location. Make sure that the location is reserved well in advance of the meeting. Establish a date and time for the meeting that is convenient for every team member. The biggest complaint from educators has to do with meetings scheduled for after-school hours. Staff want to know who is going to pay them for the time they put in. Generally, this argument can be countered by reminding education professionals that they are professionals and, as such, they must invest their time in creating a professional environment that supports their beliefs and values. If they, as professionals, do not fix the problem, someone else will, and they may not like the solution. When this argument is raised, it may be a good idea to ask the participants to list what it means to them as individuals and to the students, district, and school for them to solve this problem. At the end of the exercise, all of the comments combined on a flip chart generally form such a long list that everyone recognizes the value in solving the problem.

Meeting Attendance

Meeting attendance is mandatory, but there may be a legitimate reason why someone cannot attend a meeting. When someone cannot attend a meeting, he or she must contact the team leader and explain the reason. When someone misses a meeting, he or she agrees to accept any task assigned by the team. If someone consistently misses meetings, he or she should be asked to resign from the team, and a replacement should be selected.

Promptness and Attention

The meeting should start and end on time. The participants should give the meeting their full attention. They should not be trying to complete another task while at the meeting. Phone calls should not be allowed except for emergencies. Distractions should be kept to a minimum. Break periods should be established at the beginning of the meeting.

Agenda and Minutes

The team should agree on the next meeting's agenda prior to the conclusion of each meeting. The team recorder should keep minutes of each meeting. The minutes of the previous meeting and the agenda for the next meeting should be sent to the team members in advance of each meeting. The minutes should reflect the tasks that have been assigned to individual members. The team recorder should keep a central file of the minutes of the team meetings. The central file should also contain the project reports submitted by team members as they conclude their projects.

Roles and Responsibilities

Generally, the team will assign specific tasks to team members. However, there may be regular duties that the team may assign to one or two members. These tasks should be assigned to the members at the initial meetings. For example, team meetings in England require afternoon tea. One person is assigned the responsibility to ensure that tea is available for the members.

Team Skill Assessment

Early in the problem-solving process, the team should determine the areas of expertise for each member of the team. This will enable the team to identify the external resource requirements that may be needed to solve the problem. For example, we are working with a high school to develop an economic resource database for the community. The team is composed of representatives from the school, the Chamber of Commerce, the community, and the student population. The team developed a list of skills for each member of the team and realized that they lacked a member with computer expertise. External resources had to be secured to complete the task.

Resource Requirements

This is a major issue that is often overlooked. Very early in the problem-solving process, the team should develop a list of resources that will be needed to resolve the problem. One of the key roles of the quality steering committee is to provide the improvement teams with the resources needed to do the job. One of the major complaints from improvement teams is that the steering committee does not respond to their requests for assistance in a timely manner. The steering committee complains that they had not been provided with sufficient notification from the improvement teams for the resources they required.

35

Project Schedule

Every team should establish a project schedule prior to beginning work. This will enable the team members to schedule the team meetings in their calendars. It will help management to understand the process the team will use to the solve the problem. It provides the team with specific milestones and objectives by which the team can measure its progress. Developing a project schedule helps the team to be efficient and eliminate wasted effort.

Communication

The team should establish a process by which the team can communicate its work to others. Team communications should summarize the team's activities. Other members of the school or district will be kept informed of the team's activities and, in many instances, can provide valuable feedback to the team. It is important for the team to remember to summarize its activities in the general report. Focus on providing others with important information. Whenever possible, use existing communication processes to keep others informed.

Characteristics of Effective Teams

Promptness

Meetings should start and end on time. Members should come to the meeting prepared to participate in the team activities. If a member is late for a meeting, he or she should quietly enter the room so as to cause minimal disruption to the meeting. At the break, the member should explain why he or she was late to the meeting. Team members should also plan on participating in the entire meeting. Unless otherwise agreed to, members should not bring food to the meetings.

Participation

Every team member is expected to participate in all of the team's activities. It is the facilitator's responsibility to ensure that no single team member dominates the discussions while others hardly speak at all. The facilitator should develop a process that ensures that everyone participates in the discussion.

Basic Conversational Courtesies

Everyone should listen attentively and respectfully to others. Team members should not interrupt each other. Only one conversation should be conducted at a time, and members should not pass notes to each other while someone is trying to speak.

Agenda and Minutes

The team recorder is responsible for keeping minutes of the meetings. The agenda should be published for every meeting and reviewed at the beginning of every meeting. The final team report should be approved by the entire team. In some instances, teams will rotate this activity among the members, although we discourage this practice. As previously stated, one of the major functions of the team is to develop a knowledge base that others can use to implement quality. Rotating this function among the team members diminishes the usefulness of the reference material.

Breaks

At the beginning of every meeting, the team should decide when and how long breaks will be. The team should break at the designated time and the team members should resume activities at the agreed time. The team will find that scheduling breaks limits the number of interruptions.

Assignments

Much of a team's work is done between meetings. When members are assigned responsibilities, it is important that they complete tasks on time. If a team member is unable to complete the task according to the schedule established by the team, he or she should bring the matter to the attention of the entire team. The team may have to assign additional resources to the task or assign the task to another team member.

Discussions

Everyone is encouraged to participate in the team's discussion. Members should not attack one another for their thoughts. It is one thing to attack the idea, but it is another to attack the person expressing the idea. People should be made to feel that their opinions are valued.

Next Meeting Agenda

At the conclusion of every meeting, the team should establish an agenda for the next meeting. The team should answer the question, "What must we accomplish next to complete the project on time?" The development of a team agenda also enhances the capability of the team. The agenda is owned by the team rather than a single individual.

Meeting Evaluation

Evaluation is the most important and difficult activity the team will undertake. Self-critique is a team's main source of feedback and the only way to avoid letting problems go unnoticed. The most convenient time for evaluation is at the end of the meeting. Another good time to evaluate a meeting is right in the middle of it. The meeting should be evaluated on two key points: effectiveness and efficiency. The meeting evaluation form provided in the Appendix can be used as a general guideline for evaluating the team's meetings. The team may decide to develop its own evaluation form.

Meeting Close

Always end the meeting on a friendly note. No one should leave the meeting feeling unappreciated. Sometimes discussions become very heated and painful. It is the facilitator's responsibility to ensure that harmony exists at the end of the meeting.

Principles of Effective Team Management

Meeting Management

The facilitator should ensure that the team's activities are governed by the principles of quality. Team meetings should also be team training sessions. A complaint often received from education professionals is that they have attended a quality training session and still do not know what to do with the information they learned. Our practice is to wrap the team meeting around a training exercise. This enables the team to immediately use the tools they are learning to solve the problem.

Team Discipline

This is a very difficult issue for the team to address. It is one of the main reasons we strongly recommend that an external facilitator be used initially to manage the team's activities. The major areas of concern are attendance, completing tasks on time, uneven work load, lack of participation at meetings, and lack of results. An external facilitator is objective and does not have a vested interest in the process or the people. Therefore, it is easier for the external facilitator to enforce team rules. Most groups fail because the group slowly disintegrates. External facilitators prevent this from happening.

Maintaining Focus

In a previous section, it was strongly recommended that the team establish a project schedule. An important check for the team is to review the progress it makes against the project schedule. This will enable the team to recognize problems that it is having in meeting its schedule and to take corrective action. It is also an opportunity for the facilitator to reinforce the importance of the task and the need to maintain a schedule.

By way of example, the quality transportation committee for a local school became bogged down in the definition of students eligible for free transportation. The law mandated one definition, the school board adopted another definition, and political interests provided another. Until the team could define the student population eligible for public transportation, it could not define the bus routes and establish a transportation budget.

The team became very frustrated because of lack of progress. Finally, the facilitator divided the team into three subteams, and each team developed a student definition, a bus route schedule, and a transportation budget. The subteam reports were presented to the entire team for review and comment. Ultimately, the team reached consensus on the definition of student eligibility, a bus route schedule, and a transportation budget. When the team presented its results to the school board for review, the board said that it did not realize the transportation costs could vary so greatly. The board finally accepted the team's recommendations for student eligibility and a transportation schedule that did not conflict with the law. The recommendations of the task team were as broad as both the school board and political definitions. The school board presented the recommendations to the community and gained community-wide support for its actions. If the facilitator had not kept the team focused, the team would not have produced any results.

Chapter 6

Tools for Reaching Consensus

Consensus is commonly defined as complete or unanimous agreement of the team. In quality, consensus has several meanings. The meaning of consensus in the quality improvement process is determined by the team's constraints. The major constraint that determines the team's definition for consensus is time. Consensus is reached when all members of a group are willing to accept a decision, even though the decision may not necessarily be an individual's first choice.

To determine consensus, the facilitator or team leader should ask:

◆ **Does everyone on the team accept the decision?** If the answer is yes, the decision has been made.

◆ **Is there any opposition to the decision?** If no one responds to the question, the answer is assumed to be no. If someone speaks up, the team must address the individual's concerns, but the individual is not allowed to stop the process.

◆ **Can everyone live with the decision?** A yes response ensures that no one has a real conflict with the decision and that everyone will support the team's decision.

The team must determine how it will reach consensus prior to initiating any activities. Once the definition of consensus is reached by the team, the definition must remain constant. According to our observations, teams will fail if the definition of consensus changes. Once established, the definition of consensus cannot be changed for any reason.

The tools and techniques explained in this section are designed to help teams work toward consensus. They are not intended to make the decision for the team. The objective of the tools and techniques is bring viewpoints, especially conflicting ones, to the surface to be addressed in an open and trusting environment. The tools will help identify team members with differing viewpoints—those to whom others should listen in order to understand why they are not in agreement. Consensus cannot be reached if team members are prevented from expressing their opinions and viewpoints.

List Reduction Technique

The list reduction technique is a way of processing the output of a brainstorming session. The objective of the list reduction technique is to clarify the options so that all team members understand them. Once the team members understand the items on the list, the list can be reduced to a manageable number.

How to Use the List Reduction Technique

Before the list of potential issues or solutions can be reduced, everyone on the team must have a clear understanding of all of the items on the list. The first activity is for the team leader to review each item with the team to eliminate any doubts. Once all of the doubts have been resolved, the team should identify some "filter" criteria that can be used for an item to remain on the list. Some of the filters that can be used to identify problem areas are:

> ◆ **Does this item (the one on the list) support the team's purpose?**
>
> ◆ **Is the item within the control or influence of the team?**
>
> ◆ **Is the problem worth solving? Will it have a major impact on improving the quality of the output?**

If the answer to any one of the questions is no, the team should remove that item from the list.

Some of the filters used for reducing the list of potential solutions are:

> ◆ **Is the solution likely to solve the problem?**
>
> ◆ **Is the solution feasible?**
>
> ◆ **Is the solution within the constraints established for the team?**
>
> ◆ **Is the solution one we can afford?**

Again, if the answer to any one of the questions is no, the team should remove that item from the list.

Keeping the agreed-upon criteria in mind, the team members vote on each item. Generally, a simple majority keeps an item on the list. The team focuses on the remaining items on the list. If a person feels very strongly about an item being removed from the list, the team should provide the individual with an opportunity to explain his or her viewpoints relative to the issue before the team makes a final decision on the item.

If the filtered list contains more than five items, the process is repeated. This time the team develops more stringent criteria. The process is continued until the list is reduced to no more than five potential solutions.

Criteria Rating Forms

Criteria rating forms are used to evaluate the relationship between problems identified during the brainstorming sessions and the team's mission. They are also used to determine the potential of solutions to resolve problems. The rating criteria is determined by the team. Criteria can be treated equally, or they can be weighted relative to each other. We strongly recommend that the criteria be rated equally to each other. In this way, the team is clear in its evaluation process.

The worksheets illustrated on the next pages are used in the following processes:

♦ **Problem selection process (criteria defined by the team)**

♦ **Solution selection process (criteria defined by the team)**

♦ **Criteria rating process for problems (criteria to be defined by the team)**

♦ **Criteria rating process for solutions (criteria to be defined by the team)**

Criteria Rating Form for Problem Selection

Problem Criteria	Problem-Statement	Problem-Statement	Problem-Statement	Problem-Statement	Problem-Statement
Can the team solve the problem?					
Is the problem important?					
Does the team have control of it?					
Has the team agreed that it is a problem they want to work on?					
Total Score					

Ranking Key:
3 = To a great extent
2 = To some extent
1 = To a slight extent

The team prioritizes the problem statements according to their ranking and continues to filter the process by using the evaluation sheets on the next pages.

Problem Selection Worksheet

Problem Statements ➡️	Problem-Statement	Problem-Statement	Problem-Statement	Problem-Statement	Problem-Statement
Solve 1 2 3 4 5 Low High					
Importance 1 2 3 4 5 Low High					
Control 1 2 3 4 5 Low High					
Difficulty 1 2 3 4 5 Low High					
Time 1 2 3 4 5 Low High					
Resources 1 2 3 4 5 Low High					

Key: In the boxes across the top, write the problem statements the team is considering. Rate each problem statement against the listed criteria by working across each row. The higher the total score, the greater the likelihood that the problem is appropriate for the team to work on.

The following definitions apply to the terms listed in the Problem Selection Worksheet:

Solve: The extent to which the team has the capability to solve the problem

Importance: The seriousness or urgency of the problem

Control: The extent to which the team controls the problem and can control the solution

Difficulty: The team's assessment about the difficulty it will encounter while working through the problem to a solution

Time: The team's assessment about the amount of time it will need to resolve the problem

Resources: The amount of internal and external resources required to solve the problem (people, release time from class, money, etc.)

Solution Selection Worksheet

Solution Statements ➡	Solution-Statement	Solution-Statement	Solution-Statement	Solution-Statement	Solution-Statement
Solve 1 2 3 4 5 Low High					
Appropriateness 1 2 3 4 5 Low High					
Control 1 2 3 4 5 Low High					
Acceptability 1 2 3 4 5 Low High					
Time 1 2 3 4 5 Low High					
Resource Availability 1 2 3 4 5 Low High					

Key: In the boxes across the top, write the solution statements the team is considering. Rate each solution statement against the listed criteria by working across each row. The higher the total score, the greater the likelihood that the solution can be effectively implemented.

The following definitions apply to the terms listed in the Solution Selection Worksheet:

Solve: The extent to which the team can implement the solution to solve the problem

Appropriateness: The degree to which the resources required to implement the solution (money, people, release time, etc.) are available to the team

Control: The extent to which the implementation of the solution is within the control of the team

Acceptability: The degree to which other administrators, teachers, staff, and stakeholder groups involved in the process will accept the solution and the changes it might impose on the department, school, or district

Time: An assessment of the length of time required to solve the problem

Resource availability: The extent to which the resources (money, people, release time, etc.) required to implement the solution are available to the team

Criteria Rating Form for Problems

Criteria and Points Weighted (if applicable) ↓ ↓		Problem-Statement	Problem-Statement	Problem-Statement	Problem-Statement	Problem-Statement
Total Score						

Ranking Key: As a group identify and define the criteria to be used in evaluating problem statements. Enter the criteria and points (e.g., 1 = low, 5 = high in the boxes on the left. Write abbreviated problem statements in the boxes across the top. Work across, the form evaluating all problem statements against the first criterion, then the second, and so forth. As an option, you may decide to assign weighting factors to some criteria. If, for example, "release time" is critical, you may wish to weight it double the other factors, multiplying its score by 2 before entering it in the grid.

Criteria Rating Form for Solutions

Criteria and Points Weighted (if applicable) ↓ ↓		Solution-Statement	Solution-Statement	Solution-Statement	Solution-Statement	Solution-Statement
Total Score						

Ranking Key: As a group identify and define the criteria to be used in evaluating potential solutions. Enter the criteria and points (e.g., 1 = low, 5 = high in the boxes on the left. Write abbreviated solution statements in the boxes across the top. Work across, the form evaluating all solution statements against the first criterion, then the second, and so forth. As an option, you may decide to assign weighting factors to some criteria. If, for example, "acceptability" is critical, you may wish to weight it double the other factors, multiplying its score by 2 before entering it in the grid.

How to Use Criteria Rating Forms

To use criteria rating forms:

♦ **Decide what factors or criteria are to be considered.**

♦ **Reach agreement on their definitions.**

♦ **Determine what, if any, weights should be assigned.**

♦ **Agree on a points scale to be used.**

♦ **Discuss each "cell" on the form to arrive at a consensus rating.**

It is best to look at all options (e.g., potential solutions) and rate them on a particular criterion (e.g., the team's ability to control the implementation) at the same time. The team may determine that Solution B provides the greatest control. Assigning it the highest value then makes it easier to assign ratings to the other portions relative to Solution B.

When to Use Criteria Rating Forms

Criteria rating forms are used:

♦ **In selecting the problem statements for the team to work on**

♦ **As a means of evaluating the potential solutions generated in the brainstorming sessions**

Weighted Voting

Weighted voting is a way to quantify the positions and preferences of team members. Weighted voting differs from criteria rating forms in three ways:

♦ **No decision factors or criteria are used.**

♦ **Individual members' votes are recorded.**

♦ **There is no discussion or effort to reach agreement on a single issue.**

How Is Weighted Voting Used?

To use the weighted voting technique, each member is given a number of votes to distribute to the various options in accordance with his or her preferences. Voting is completed on the Weighted Voting Form. Generally, the number of votes given each member is about one-and-a-half times the number of options. Team members decide how to distribute their votes among the options to indicate their relative preferences. After the team members have completed their individual forms, a team weighted voting chart is recorded on a flip chart, and the combined point totals are allocated to each solution.

Weighted Voting Form

Team Members ↓ ↓	Option-Statement	Option-Statement	Option-Statement	Option-Statement	Option-Statement

Helpful Hints

♦ Encourage the team members to allocate points to each solution.

♦ Have the team members agree on the voting scale to be used (e.g., 3 = high, 2 = medium, 1 = low) before any votes are taken.

♦ Ask the team members to show their votes for each option all at once by sharing their forms with the rest of the team.

♦ Ask for and record votes by option instead of by person.

Weighted voting does not make decisions for the team. It merely gives the team information about where individual team members stand and how strongly they feel. This information makes it easier for opposing viewpoints to surface. Consensus cannot be reached without dealing with those viewpoints.

When to Use Weighted Voting

Weighted voting is most useful for "taking the temperature" of the team as it works to identify problem areas and potential solutions. The approach can be used to identify the group's positions and priorities.

Chapter 7

Basic Tools of Quality

Quality management is founded upon the principle of collecting and using data to define and analyze the problem. Decisions are based on the data. We have helped educational leaders to use TQM tools and techniques to collect, analyze, and understand relevant data. However, TQM is **not** tools and techniques. TQM tools and techniques only **assist** in the quality transformation of a school or district. Unfortunately, too many people believe that TQM is merely tools and techniques. These people are destined to fail in TQM efforts.

The following matrices depict typical uses of TQM tools and techniques.

TQM Basic Tools Matrix

TOOLS:	PROBLEM DEFINITION	PROBLEM ANALYSIS	DATA COLLECTION	DATA ANALYSIS	SOLUTION DEVELOPMENT	SOLUTION IMPLEMENTATION	SOLUTION ASSESSMENT
BRAINSTORMING - BRAINWRITING Team members discuss ideas on the issue. Brainwriting is like Brainstorming only people write their ideas down on paper and the paper is collected at the end of the session and the ideas are listed on a flip chart.	X	X					
FLOW CHARTS	X	X	X		X	X	X
CHECKSHEETS			X		X	X	
PARETO DIAGRAMS		X		X			X
CAUSE & EFFECT DIAGRAM		X	X		X		

TQM Basic Tools Matrix

TOOLS:	PROBLEM DEFINITION	PROBLEM ANALYSIS	DATA COLLECTION	DATA ANALYSIS	SOLUTION DEVELOPMENT	SOLUTION IMPLEMENTATION	SOLUTION ASSESSMENT
GRAPHS	X	X		X			X
CONTROL CHART		X		X			X
HISTOGRAM		X		X			X
SCATTER DIAGRAM		X		X			X
TIMELINES (WHO WHAT WHEN (WEEKS))		X	X		X		

TQM Basic Tools Matrix

TOOLS:	PROBLEM DEFINITION	PROBLEM ANALYSIS	DATA COLLECTION	DATA ANALYSIS	SOLUTION DEVELOPMENT	SOLUTION IMPLEMENTATION	SOLUTION ASSESSMENT
FORCE FIELD ANALYSIS Supporting Opposing Culture → ← Tradition Society → ← Fear Work → ← Control Market →		**X**			**X**		
AFFINITY DIAGRAM **Barriers** **Facilitators** • Finances • Training • Knowledge • Support • Time • Teams						**X**	**X**
PROCESS MODELING PROCESS INPUT OUTPUT	**X**	**X**			**X**	**X**	**X**

Flowcharts

The example illustrated below is a **detailed flowchart**. A flowchart is a diagram of the steps in a process. Flowcharting prevents the team from leapfrogging over activities that are natural steps in the process. By showing how the process works, the team can identify potential problem areas and create a new and improved process. Flowcharting is useful in the process of thinking through a new process before it is implemented so that potential problems can be easily avoided.

Detailed Flowchart

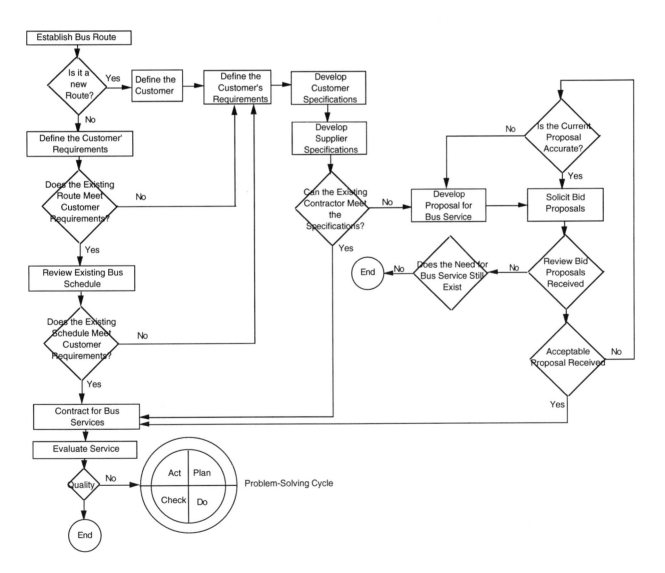

In the example on the preceding page, the team used this detailed flowchart to diagram the sequence to develop bus routes. This chart shows all of the stages that the process must follow before the district establishes a bus route. The questions most frequently asked by participants at workshops are, "How complicated does the flowchart have to be?" and "Are there standard international symbols to use when developing a flowchart?" The flowchart can be as simple or as complicated as it needs to be. Knowledge of the problem area will determine how complex the flowchart is. One of the tools used to develop a flowchart is brainstorming. In brainstorming, the group lists the steps in the process and puts them in sequential order.

We have not found any international standards for the symbols used in flowcharts. Computer programmers use flowcharts to depict how their computer applications run. I have used flowcharts to develop COBOL computer programs. The symbols used in this exercise are the symbols used to develop computer flowcharts. The standard symbols are a diamond to represent a decision, a circle to represent the end of process, and a rectangle to represent a function.

Another example of a flowchart is the **top-down flowchart**, depicted on the next page. The top-down flowchart is easy to use, and students generally find that it is a great tool to use to plan their homework activities.

Top-Down Flowchart

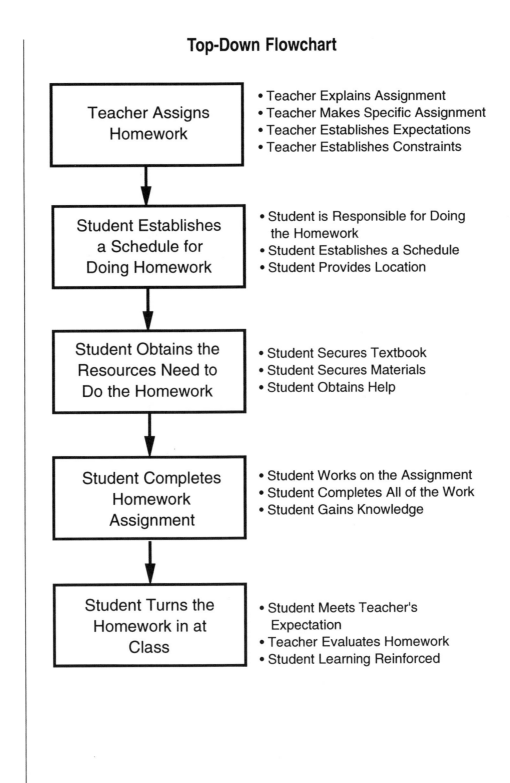

Teacher Assigns Homework	• Teacher Explains Assignment • Teacher Makes Specific Assignment • Teacher Establishes Expectations • Teacher Establishes Constraints
Student Establishes a Schedule for Doing Homework	• Student is Responsible for Doing the Homework • Student Establishes a Schedule • Student Provides Location
Student Obtains the Resources Need to Do the Homework	• Student Secures Textbook • Student Secures Materials • Student Obtains Help
Student Completes Homework Assignment	• Student Works on the Assignment • Student Completes All of the Work • Student Gains Knowledge
Student Turns the Homework in at Class	• Student Meets Teacher's Expectation • Teacher Evaluates Homework • Student Learning Reinforced

Checksheets

Checksheets are excellent tools for recording data. In the far left-hand column are listed the items against which the groups will be assessed. Generally, a check or tick mark indicates that the task is completed or that the item is secured. It is a very simple and quick way to keep track of students, books, or supplies. The attendance sheet in school is an example of a checksheet.

ITEM	GROUP A	GROUP B	GROUP C	GROUP D	GROUP E	GROUP F	GROUP G

Pareto Charts

The Pareto chart enables careful analysis of information, so that the factors that require attention can be identified. The Pareto chart is basically a bar chart in which factors in a process are shown in descending order of importance or frequency. In the example below, the Pareto chart was used by a teacher–student team to study the reasons for excessive student absence from class. The team found that the vast majority of absences were due to illness. Therefore, they focused their attention on instituting a student health-care program that focused on illness prevention. The end result was a dramatic decrease in the number of students who were absent from class due to illness. When the teacher–student team completed the health-care program, they began to focus on the other causes of student absences. The team worked with a local charity to obtain proper clothing for students from poor families. As a result, the number of students absent from school because of dress and attitude also decreased. As a result of this project, the total number of student absences was significantly reduced.

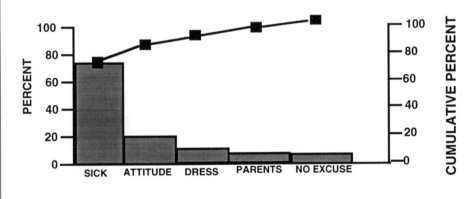

REASONS FOR STUDENT ABSENCES

Cause-and-Effect Diagrams

The cause-and-effect diagram, or the fishbone diagram (because of its shape) is an excellent tool. It is helpful in determining the root causes and effects within a school or district's processes and systems. The cause-and-effect diagram can be used to identify the components in the process responsible for an existing problem. We use the cause-and-effect diagram to plan new processes more effectively and efficiently. This helps to ensure that the program meets our customer's requirements the first time.

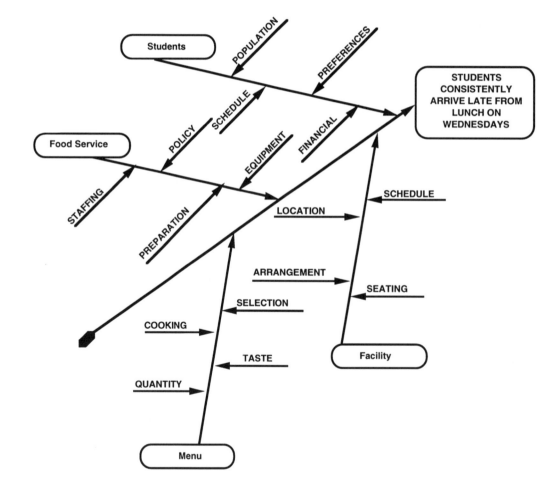

As a tool, the cause-and-effect diagram is used to analyze a problem. The problem the team wants to study is described in the large box at the head of the arrow. In our example, the team at a school wants to eliminate the problems that are causing the students to consistently arrive late from lunch on Wednesdays. On the main bones of the fish, the team listed the major factors that can contribute to the outcome. The team determined that the facility, menu, food service, and students were possibly the major causes of the problem. On the little bones, the team listed the factors that could possibly contribute to the major factors that ultimately lead to the current outcome. After reviewing this process, the team determined that the policy established by the principal was responsible for the problem. The students had complained to the principal that the hamburgers they received on Wednesdays were always served cold. The principal instructed the food service staff to "cook the burgers to order." This change in policy resulted in a outcome that was unacceptable to the school. To correct the problem, the team recommended and the school purchased food warmers to keep the hamburgers at an acceptable temperature.

Graphs

A graph is a simple tool to use. It is easy to understand, because it provides a visual comparison. The following graph compares the increase in the gross price index (G.P.I.) to the total increase in education spending from 1984 to 1988. The vertical axis is the monetary measurement; the horizontal axis is the time measurement. This graph demonstrates that the growth in the cost of education has significantly exceeded the growth in the G.P.I. The G.P.I. reflects the effect of inflation and price increases on the cost of consumer goods and services.

Education Costs

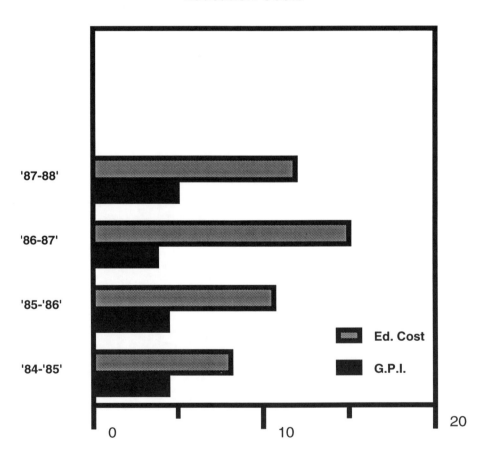

Control Charts

The control chart is used to graphically display the variation in an ongoing process. The horizontal axis is used to track time, and the vertical axis is used to track the process under review. If the process goes outside the lower control limits, it is considered "out of statistical control." This is a warning that the system needs to be adjusted or brought back into control.

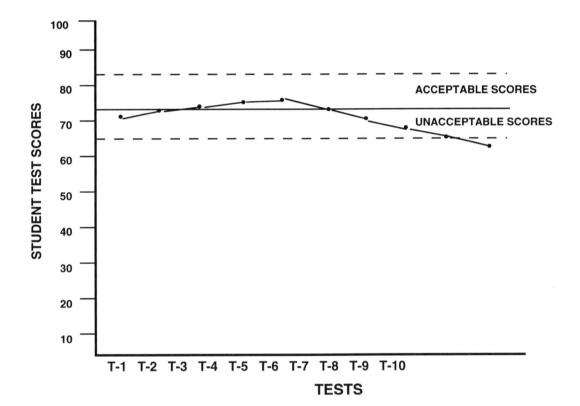

In this example, the control chart is used by students to track their test scores. In this instance, the students adopted a goal of increasing their average test scores from 68 points to 75 points. The students established 75 points as their point of reference. Test scores that went below the solid line (75 points) indicated that the student did not understand the material and that extra attention was needed in these areas. In this case, exceeding the upper limit was "good," and although it is technically out of statistical control, it is acceptable. This is one of the first tools that students can be taught to use so that they can track their academic progress. It has helped many students to improve their grades.

Histograms

We have developed a system to determine the phases of quality in a school or a district. The vehicle used to graphically demonstrate the phases of quality is a histogram. A histogram is a bar chart representation of the spread or dispersion of data. The following histogram shows that phases of quality for the administrators and teachers in this district are between the control and awareness phases. We use this tool to develop a TQM implementation plan for schools with which we work.

Phases of Quality Histogram

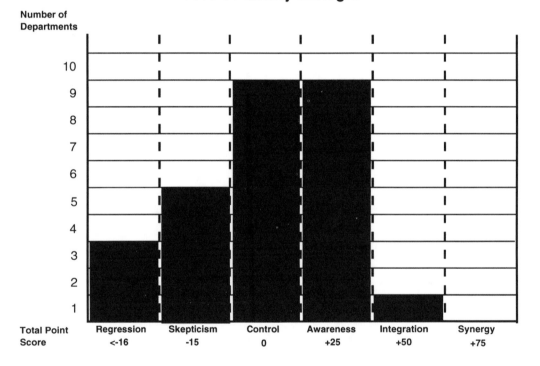

| Total Point Score | Regression <-16 | Skepticism -15 | Control 0 | Awareness +25 | Integration +50 | Synergy +75 |

Our phases of quality assessment really measures people's receptivity to change. In this example, the histogram shows the phases of quality for the 21 departments within the district. Of the 21 departments assessed, only 13 departments were receptive to quality. The remaining departments resisted every attempt to include them in the quality transformation. An extensive training and support program had to be developed for the departments that initially resisted the quality movement.

Scatter Diagrams

A scatter diagram is used to study the possible relationship between one variable and another. Occasionally, the scatter diagram is used to test for possible cause-and-effect relationships. A scatter diagram is created by setting up the horizontal axis to represent the measurement or value of one variable. The vertical axis represents the measurements of the second variable. The scatter diagram should only be used with fifty or more paired variables. Data comparison of less than fifty paired variables is of little, if any, value. Frankly, in the four years that we have been implementing TQM in education, the scatter diagram was used on only two occasions.

The plotted points form a cluster pattern. The direction and closeness of the cluster indicates the strength of the relationship between variable 1 and variable 2. The more the cluster resembles a straight line, the stronger the relationship between the variables.

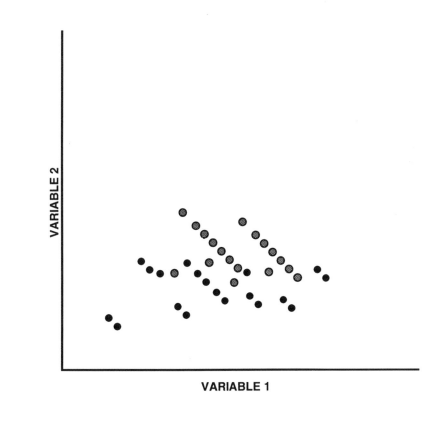

Timeline Charts

A timeline chart is an excellent project management tool. It allows you to track assignments and to develop milestones against which the project's progress can be measured. We use a computer-based project management system to manage our school projects. However, simpler timeline charts are easy to draw and simple to use. Students use them to track their progress in completing school projects. In the example below, Johnson is going to develop a flowchart of the school central admissions process. The team determined that Johnson needed approximately two weeks to complete the task. The team assigned Smith the task of surveying students, and that task is projected to take approximately one-and-one-half weeks. The timeline chart enables the team to establish project milestones and objectives. It is an effective tool to use to keep the team focused and on track.

INDIVIDUAL	TASK	PROJECT DURATION								
JOHNSON	Flow Chart Admissions Process									
SMITH	Survey Students									
PHILLIPS	Examine Other Admission Systems									

Force Field Analysis

We constantly use force field analysis to identify the factors that oppose change and those that push for change. By weighing the factors on both sides, a plan can be developed to effectively counterbalance the negative factors. Use of this tool helps to ensure the success of every quality project. In the example below, a local high school developed a force field analysis for adopting quality in schools. The students listed the driving forces that demand more from education and those forces that oppose any change in the system. The major force opposing change is fear. When developing a quality culture, a support system must be developed for those individuals who are opposed to change. Once these individuals understand what quality in education really means, they become the strongest proponents of the program.

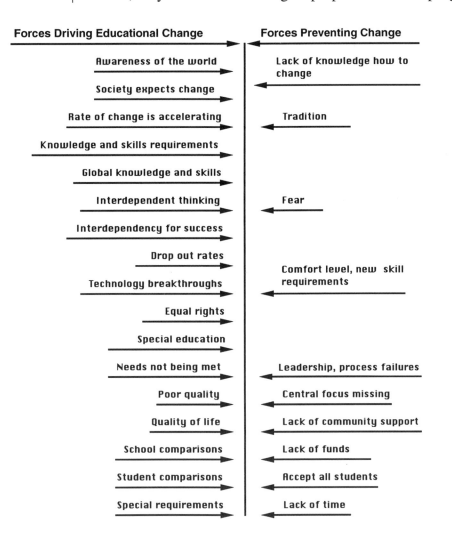

Affinity Diagrams

An affinity diagram is a simple process that is used to categorize elements of a process that have a natural link with one another. The affinity diagram is similar to a force field analysis. The affinity diagram is a tool used to develop the cause-and-effect diagram and to evaluate the force field analysis. Both tools are simple to use. In each instance, the barriers or opposing forces are listed on one side, and the positive or moving forces are listed on the other side. Both tools are extremely valuable in developing an implementation plan. The affinity diagram and force field analysis help to anticipate conflict. Once the areas where conflict is most likely to arise have been identified, a plan can be developed to minimize or eliminate the causes of conflict.

BARRIERS	FACILITATORS
• FINANCES • TIME • LACK OF UNDERSTANDING • CYNICISM: JUST ANOTHER PROGRAM • BUSINESS APPLICATION	• CANNOT AFFORD NOT TO DO • HELPS YOU DO YOUR JOB BETTER • TRAINING AVAILABLE • CULTURAL TRANSFORMATION • APPLIES EQUALLY TO SCHOOLS

Process Modeling

Process modeling is sometimes called functional modeling. Process modeling depicts the actual work process and is used to analyze complex processes. In the following example, the teacher developed a process model of the Student Services organization for a school in England. This approach enabled the teacher to understand the natural progression in the work flow for a new student entering the college. A process model is an effective tool to identify the customer/supplier chain. It enables determination of customer requirements and translation of those customer requirements into supplier specifications. Process modeling is also an effective tool to measure the cost of quality. It allows a complex process to be divided into smaller processes that can be evaluated and measured.

Functional Overview of Student Services

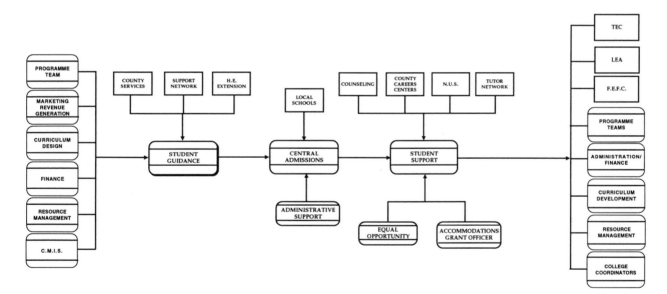

Team Conclusion

Many schools forget the process of concluding the team's activities. Once a team has completed its assignment, there is no longer a reason for the team to exist. Some schools establish permanent teams. These teams go from one task to the next task. However, permanent teams tend to build barriers within the system. People who are not part of the team begin to look suspiciously at those who are on the team. The team's work becomes suspect because the process is not open to everyone. One school indicated that its school improvement program was discontinued because it became a clique. A quality focus helps to eliminate this problem.

The following are guidelines that teams should follow after the completion of their tasks.

Recognition

The team should be recognized for its contribution. It is important to make it clear that the entire team is being recognized for the contribution that the team made. No one individual should be singled out for special recognition. Recognition can be in many forms. Although recognition often equals money, it is strongly recommended that financial rewards not be given. Rewards should be a simple expression of the school or district's gratitude for the work the team completed.

Self-Reflection

The team should perform a self-evaluation. This is a difficult task, but it is a necessary step in the quality process. Basically, what the team and others want to know is what worked, what did not work, what the team could have done differently, what management could have done to support the team more, and what was learned from the team. One of the goals of teams is to build a knowledge base of experience from which others can learn.

Standards

Once the task has been completed, the team should establish a standard for the way the process will be performed in the future. Quality is about standards. Standards enable improvement. A standard helps people to understand what is expected of them. Standards identify the way to perform a task. Standards make roles and responsibilities clearer, eliminate confusion, minimize the potential for error, and eliminate waste. They are the means by which schools can increase efficiency and productivity and reduce cost while improving the quality of education.

Assessment and Documentation

The final task the team has to complete is to assess and measure the results of its activities. Did the team accomplish what was expected of it? Whenever possible, the team should establish a monetary value for the time it spent on the task and the financial benefits realized by the school or district. Once the team assesses its activities, the team documents the processes and tools it used to complete the task. The school or district should adopt standardized forms for this process.

Chapter 8

5 + 5 Quality Team's Initiative

The 5 + 5 Quality Initiative is a program that reinforces the principles of quality on both a district-wide and school-wide basis. The 5 + 5 Quality Initiative is a process that helps the district or schools obtain total participation in the quality transformation. The program is driven by staff on both an individual and departmental basis. Every department participates in the program. Initially, only individual or departmental projects are considered for the 5 + 5 Quality Initiative. As more staff become familiar with the principles of quality and the implementation of quality tools and techniques, school-wide or district-wide projects are undertaken.

The 5 + 5 Quality Initiative is directed by the staff. It encourages every staff member to find new ways of working that increase productivity, cost effectiveness, and service quality. Staff identify program or system changes that result in both a 5% reduction in cost and a 5% percent improvement in service quality. **Only projects that accomplish both of these objectives are considered for the 5 + 5 Quality Initiative.** Every program or system change is considered. No change is too small!

Prior to implementation of the 5 + 5 Quality Initiative, staff are asked to establish a target for the number of projects that their department will implement during the school year. Team building and group consensus techniques are used to establish the 5 + 5 Quality Initiative goals for the department. **Departments should not be overly aggressive in the establishment of their goals and targets.**

What Are the Objectives of the 5 + 5 Quality Initiative?

The objectives of the 5 + 5 Quality Initiative are to:

- ◆ **Attain total participation in the district or school's quality initiative**

- ◆ **Expand the sphere of influence for the principles of quality**

- ◆ **Help staff demonstrate the added value of the quality initiative**

- ◆ **Increase the cost effectiveness and quality of all programs and services**

- ◆ **Train all staff in the implementation of quality tools and techniques**

- ◆ **Assist in the systemic change process for the district or school**

- ◆ **Provide positive feedback to staff**

- ◆ **Remove the barriers that prevent all staff from participating in the quality initiative**

The 5 + 5 Quality Initiative is used as a training tool to help all staff adopt a quality philosophy. The focus of the initiative is on both the internal and external customers. The goals for the 5 + 5 Quality Initiative are to increase customer satisfaction and to improve the cost effectiveness of the department's products and services.

This initiative does not focus on money. However, the real world of education today stresses that all staff must learn how to do more with less. The days of unlimited budget increases are gone. This program helps all staff to develop a new spending paradigm that focuses on both the cost effectiveness and the quality of the product or service. Every district or school is being asked to make very difficult funding decisions. As the 5 + 5 Quality Initiative is implemented, the school or district is better able to use its limited resources to meet the needs of students, staff, and the community.

The 5 + 5 Quality Initiative focuses on the number of programs that an individual or department can implement during a fixed time. The program focuses on system or process changes to an existing work task that results in a 5% increase in cost effectiveness and a 5% increase in service quality. Each program must increase both the cost effectiveness and quality of the product or service. The driving principle for the 5 + 5 Quality Initiative is the number of projects implemented and **not** the cost savings realized by the district or school. It is important to stress that no system or process change is too small! Every system or process change should be considered!

Does the 5 + 5 Quality Initiative Introduce Competition into the Environment?

The answer to this question is both yes and no. **Not all competition is bad.** If used properly, competition can be used to encourage people to participate in the district or school's quality initiative. This is especially true for the staff members who are perceived as barriers to the quality transformation. The competition introduced into the environment by the 5 + 5 Quality Initiative is classified as positive competition. It is positive competition because everyone is adhering to the same principles.

No department or individual is forced to participate in the 5 + 5 Quality Initiative. If a department or individual elects not to participate in the program, no punitive action is taken against the department or individual. Competition is usually the catalyst that compels people or organizations to participate in a program. No one is forced to participate in the 5 + 5 Quality Initiative. However, the lack of participation is evident to everyone.

What Are the Staff's Roles in the 5 + 5 Quality Initiative?

Staff is defined as every employee of the school or district. **The superintendent is the coach who encourages people to participate in the 5 + 5 Quality Initiative.** The superintendent tracks and reports to the school board the progress that the staff has made in achieving the objectives of the 5 + 5 Quality Initiative. The superintendent ensures that no individual or department is punished for not participating in the 5 + 5 Quality Initiative.

The administrators and managers are the departmental coaches and facilitators for the 5 + 5 Quality Initiative. Administrators and managers work with their staff to identify projects for the initiative. They track the department's progress in achieving the goals of the 5 + 5 Quality Initiative. Administrators and managers strive to remove the organizational barriers that prevent all staff from being successful. They strive to provide all staff with the legitimate and reasonable resources needed to achieve the objectives of the project.

Teachers and support staff are active participants. They are the "idea generators" for the 5 + 5 Quality Initiative. Teachers and support staff work with their department heads and managers to identify the projects that they as individuals or departmental team members will implement to achieve the objectives of the 5 + 5 Quality Initiative. Although individual contributions to the program are recognized, staff are encouraged to participate in departmental team activities.

The school board recognizes all staff for their efforts and contributions to the 5 + 5 Quality Initiative. It is the responsibility of the school board to ensure that all projects are viewed equally. This is a very difficult task. School board members tend to recognize those projects that provide the district with the greatest financial benefits. This trap must be avoided. School board members must focus on the objectives of the 5 + 5 Quality Initiative and not on the financial results. School board members must reinforce the concept that no change is too small. Every change that increases cost effectiveness and service quality by 5% is welcomed.

How Are the Results Measured?

Every project will result in either direct or indirect cost savings. **Direct cost savings are the savings in real dollars.** Direct cost savings are "hard" and measurable. For example, if a teacher spends a certain amount of money to copy material for her class and then implements a process change that reduces the cost, this is a direct cost saving. It can be measured and is reflected in the budget.

People tend to overlook indirect cost savings. Indirect cost savings are more difficult to measure but they are just as important as direct cost savings. **Indirect cost savings are the "soft" savings realized from a system or process change.** For example, it initially took two staff members three hours each to process the payroll. The system change eliminated one person from the process. There were no direct cost savings because the person is now working on other tasks. There are, however, indirect savings for the district (one person's salary for three hours). The indirect cost savings help the school or district to become more productive.

Progress is also measured by improvements in customer satisfaction. The goal of the 5 + 5 Quality Initiative is to increase customer satisfaction by 5%. Increases in customer satisfaction must be achieved by improving the quality of the product or service and by eliminating customer complaints. For example, improvements in customer satisfaction can be measured by the amount of time taken to process a request, the number of complaints received from parents or students, and by developing products or services that better meet the customer's requirements.

How Is Progress Tracked?

Graphs are displayed in each department to indicate the projects undertaken and the benefits realized. Individual staff member names are not included on the graphs. Only the projects are listed, and the benefits for the project are tracked. The graph on the next page depicts the improvements in a special education class.

Special Education Department 5 + 5 Quality Initiative Graph

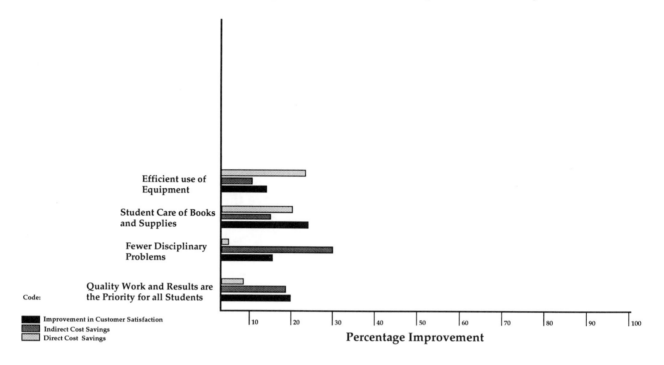

The graph depicted above lists the 5 + 5 Quality Initiative projects implemented in a special education class. This graph was maintained by both the department manager and the teacher. It was used as a tool to encourage other staff to participate in the initiative.

The percentage of improvement, listed across the bottom of the graph, is the only measurement that is displayed on the graph. **Only the individual and department know the actual direct and indirect savings achieved from the project.** Once the project has achieved the minimum goals of the 5 + 5 Quality Initiative, the department manager documents the activities undertaken and the benefits achieved. He or she then forwards the documentation to the superintendent, who reviews the documentation for accuracy and includes the project on the district-wide graph. The project forms provided in the Appendix are used to track the project and to document the project's results for the district. A copy of all the forms is forwarded to the superintendent's offices. The department continues to track the project's success until the end of the school year, when completed statistics are forwarded to the superintendent.

The superintendent is responsible for maintaining a district-wide graph that depicts all the district's 5 + 5 Quality Initiative projects. The superintendent also keeps a separate graph that depicts the direct and indirect cost savings realized from the 5 + 5 Quality Initiative projects for the district. The graph depicted below is maintained by the superintendent, and it depicts all the 5 + 5 Quality Initiative projects.

District-Wide 5 + 5 Quality Initiative Graph

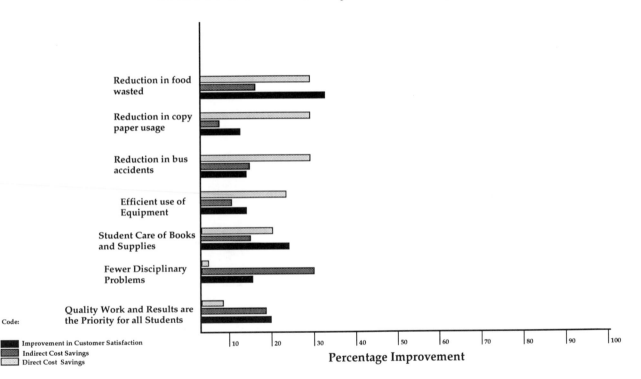

Again, the district-wide or school-wide graph does not focus on money. It focuses on the number of projects completed by the district or school's staff. This approach minimizes the potential for conflict to develop between departments and it provides positive comments for the departments and staff participating in the program.

The district-wide 5 + 5 Quality Initiative cost savings graph depicted below is used to document the total direct and indirect cost savings realized by the district. Only the total financial savings are shown on the graph. Projects are not listed, individuals participating on the project team are not identified, and departments are not recognized for their contributions.

District-Wide 5 + 5 Quality Initiative Cost Savings Graph

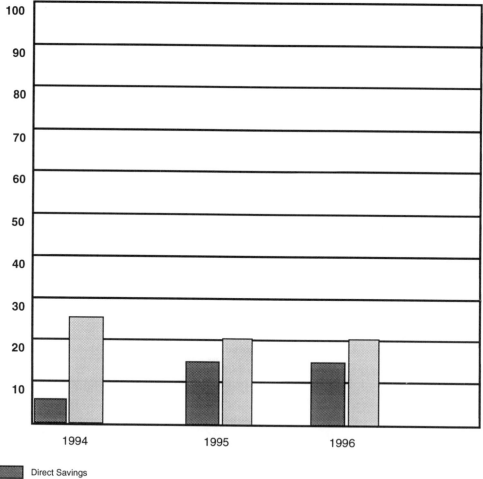

In the graph illustrated on the previous page, the district decided to track the cost savings that the district would realize from the 5 + 5 Quality Initiative projects for three years. Generally, savings realized in the initial year of the project will provide the district with cost benefits in subsequent years. It is not necessary to project future cost savings for the district. However, it is necessary to depict the current cost savings. This graph clearly demonstrates the financial benefits of the quality initiative for the school or district.

Why Should the Staff Participate in the 5 + 5 Quality Initiative?

There are several reasons why the staff should participate in the 5 + 5 Quality Initiative. More and more pressure is being applied to education by society to reduce educational budgets. This pressure is not going to go away. The 5 + 5 Quality Initiative is a program that schools can use to cope with these pressures.

Additionally, staff constantly ask for more funds to develop new and innovative learning programs. Many of these projects cannot be implemented because of budget constraints. In many instances, the school board agrees to share the cost savings with the staff. Generally, one-half of the savings goes directly to the district, and one half is used by staff to develop new programs, purchase equipment, attend professional development seminars, or for other similar activities. The success of the 5 + 5 Quality Initiative makes funding for these activities possible.

In some districts, the 5 + 5 Quality Initiative is used to identify program savings that will eliminate the need to reduce staff. The superintendent is faced with making many difficult staffing recommendations. On occasion, staff have stated that they should be provided with the opportunity to reduce program costs before positions are eliminated. This program provides them with that opportunity.

Chapter 9

Conclusion

The success of quality teams does not just depend on the effective application of TQM tools and techniques. Of greater importance is effective team participation. This book has provided an overview of the approach we use to develop effective teams. A major obstacle to the creation of an effective team is fear. If fear and distrust exist in the environment, the people within that environment are not willing to take risks or be innovative.

The development of a quality culture begins and ends with learning. An extensive TQM training program is required for any program to succeed. Teams should have access to the best available training aids, whether books, videos, audiotapes, articles, or trainers. Training helps the team to develop trust and self-confidence. It is essential that the teams have the support of management and that management is willing to allow the teams to fail. Failing is a learning process, and quality is all about learning.

Reference Guide

The Quality Tools and Techniques Reference Guide (see next page) is used to illustrate when to apply the tools and techniques of quality to the quality improvement process. It is only a guide. Each school may develop its own reference guide. The tools and techniques of quality are flexible. They can be applied to almost any step in the quality improvement process. The application of the tools and techniques to the quality improvement process depicted in the reference guide are based on our experience and the experiences of other education professionals.

89

Quality Tools and Techniques Reference Guide

Tool	Organizing Teams	Managing Team Meetings	Team Code of Conduct	Monitoring Team Activities	Team Roles and Responsibilities	Evaluating Team Meetings	Measuring Team Effectiveness	Documenting Team Activities	Collecting Data	Analyzing Data	Selecting Team Activities	Identification of Constraints	Developing a Solution	Implementing a Solution	Assessing Results	Developing Standards	Documenting Results	Gaining Consensus
Team Management Tools																		
Meeting Planner Guide	●	●	●					●			●		●					●
Goal Sheet	●	●	●	●	●	●	●	●			●	●				●	●	
Team Focus and Direction Model	●	●		●	●	●	●	●			●	●		●		●	●	
Constraints Classification Form		●		●		●		●			●	●				●	●	
Roles & Responsibilities Chart	●	●	●	●	●	●	●	●			●	●	●	●		●	●	
Team Effectiveness Chart	●	●	●	●	●	●	●	●	●	●	●	●	●			●	●	
Meeting Evaluation Form		●	●	●		●	●									●	●	
Tools for Generating Ideas																		
Brainwriting		●		●	●	●			●	●	●		●			●	●	
Brainstorming	●		●	●		●			●	●	●		●				●	
Tools for Collecting Data																		
Checksheets	●	●	●	●	●	●	●	●	●	●	●			●			●	
Interviewing									●		●	●	●		●	●		
Surveying								●	●		●	●	●		●	●		
Tools for Reaching Consensus																		
List Reduction		●		●					●	●	●		●		●	●	●	
Criteria Rating Forms	●	●		●	●				●	●	●		●		●	●	●	
Weighted Voting				●					●	●	●		●		●	●	●	
Paired Comparisons									●	●	●		●		●	●	●	
Multi-Voting Form		●		●					●	●	●		●		●	●	●	
Tools for Displaying & Analyzing Data																		
Cause-and-Effect Diagram				●		●	●	●	●	●	●	●	●		●	●	●	
Force Field Analysis				●			●		●	●			●	●	●			
Histogram										●	●	●					●	
Time Charts	●	●					●	●			●		●	●	●			
Pareto Analysis				●		●			●	●	●		●	●	●		●	
Flowcharts								●	●	●			●	●	●	●	●	
Control Charts				●		●	●			●			●	●	●	●	●	
Affinity Diagram				●		●			●	●			●	●	●			●
Process Modeling										●	●		●	●	●	●	●	
Scatter Diagram									●	●	●		●	●	●	●	●	

Quality Terms

The following TQM terms are used in education:

♦   **Output:**   A product or service produced as part of a job and passed on to the next person in the work process. For example:

> **Output**
>
> Attendance sheets
>
> Grade forms
>
> Requisitions

♦   **Customer:**   The next person or group in the work process; the receiver of the output produced. For example:

Output	Customer
Attendance sheets	Secretary
Grade forms	Central office
Requisitions	Secretary

♦   **Internal customer:**   The next person or group in the work process that is within the organization or work group.

♦   **External customer:**   The next person or group that receives the output that is external to the organization or work group.

♦   **Primary customer:**   The next person or group in the work process that receives the output.

♦ **Secondary customer:** Other customers, beyond the next in the process, who receive or make use of the output produced.

Output	Primary customer	Secondary customer(s)
Attendance sheets	Secretary	Parents
		Administration
Grade forms	Central office	Students
		Parents
		Administration
Requisitions	Secretary	Purchasing
		Budgeting
		Department head

♦ **End user:** The consumer or final customer who makes use of the final output. For example:

Process	End user(s)
K-12 education	Society, business, higher education, etc.

♦ **Supplier:** The individual or group responsible for producing the output. The supplier is also the individual or group from whom raw material is received. A person can be both a customer and a supplier. For example:

Supplier	Customer
7th grade teacher	8th grade teacher
6th grade teacher	7th grade teacher

♦ **Requirements:** What the customer wants, needs, or expects of the output in order to do his or her job. Customer requirements may be general, but they should be made specific. For example:

Output	Requirements
Attendance sheet	Must be legible
	Must be in the office by 8:00 a.m.
	Must be completed daily
Grade forms	Must be numeric
	Must be turned in by a specific date
Requisitions	Typed in triplicate
	One copy to central office
	One copy to purchasing
	One copy for file

♦ **Specifications:** Translation of customer requirements into a detailed description of the output based on the customer's requirements. For example:

Customer requirement	Specifications
Presentation by administrators to superintendent of schools relative to the adoption of goals and objectives for the academic year	90-minute presentation with up to 10 transparencies covering all points
	Presenter: Jerry
	30 minutes for Q&A
	Ready by Friday

♦ **Measurement:** A systematic plan for collecting information about the quality of the output. Measurements should accomplish the following:

> ♦ **Provide early identification of potential problems**
>
> ♦ **Be used as a problem prevention tool**
>
> ♦ **Permit objective evaluation of the quality of the output**

♦ **Customer/supplier chain:** Identification of the relationships between the customer and the supplier. It is used to identify the customer requirements and to establish supplier specifications.

Worksheets

5 + 5 Worksheets

Project Description

> **Briefly describe the project:**

Current Process

> **Briefly describe how the process is currently performed:**

Process Changes

> **Briefly describe the process or system changes that will be initiated to improve cost effectiveness and service quality by 5%:**

Project Measurements

> **Identify the measurements that you will use to determine the direct and indirect savings and the improvement in service quality.**
>
> **Direct Savings:**
>
> **Indirect Savings:**

Service Quality Improvements:

Project Results

Describe the results realized from this project. How were the cost savings realized? How was service quality improvement measured?

Results

Report financial results below:

Appendix

Master Forms

Team Assessment Matrix

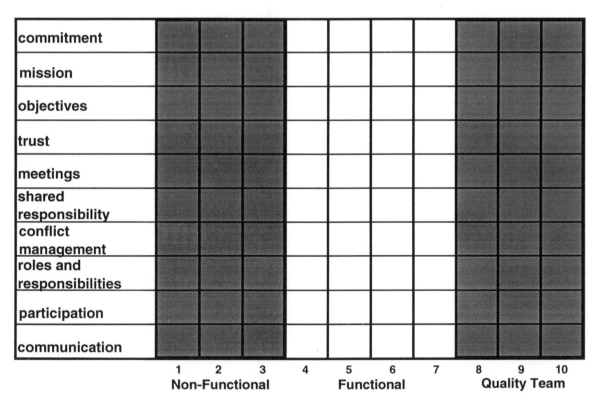

	1	2	3	4	5	6	7	8	9	10
commitment										
mission										
objectives										
trust										
meetings										
shared responsibility										
conflict management										
roles and responsibilities										
participation										
communication										

Non-Functional   Functional   Quality Team

Team Organization Assessment Matrix

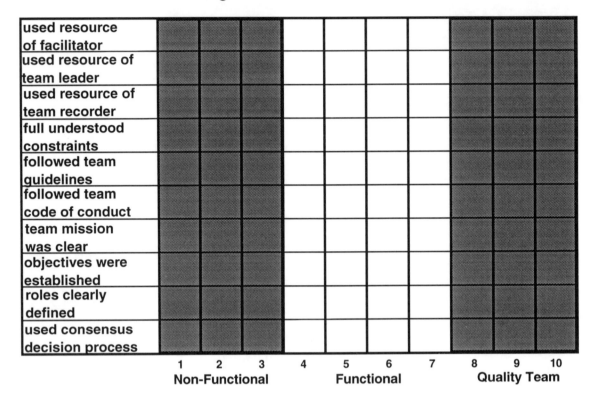

	1	2	3	4	5	6	7	8	9	10
used resource of facilitator										
used resource of team leader										
used resource of team recorder										
full understood constraints										
followed team guidelines										
followed team code of conduct										
team mission was clear										
objectives were established										
roles clearly defined										
used consensus decision process										

Non-Functional   Functional   Quality Team

Criteria Rating Form for Problem Selection

Problem Criteria	Problem-Statement	Problem-Statement	Problem-Statement	Problem-Statement	Problem-Statement
Can the team solve the problem?					
Is the problem important?					
Does the team have control of it?					
Has the team agreed that it is a problem they want to work on?					
Total Score					

Ranking Key:
3 = To a great extent
2 = To some extent
1 = To a slight extent

Problem Selection Worksheet

Problem Statements →	Problem-Statement	Problem-Statement	Problem-Statement	Problem-Statement
Solve 1 2 3 4 5 Low High				
Importance 1 2 3 4 5 Low High				
Control 1 2 3 4 5 Low High				
Difficulty 1 2 3 4 5 Low High				
Time 1 2 3 4 5 Low High				
Resources 1 2 3 4 5 Low High				

Key: In the boxes across the top, write the problem statements the team is considering. Rate each problem statement against the listed criteria by working across each row. The higher the total score, the greater the likelihood that the problem is appropriate for the team to work on.

Solution Selection Worksheet

Solution Statements ⟶	Solution-Statement	Solution-Statement	Solution-Statement	Solution-Statement	Solution-Statement	Solution-Statement
Solve 1 2 3 4 5 Low High						
Appropriateness 1 2 3 4 5 Low High						
Control 1 2 3 4 5 Low High						
Acceptability 1 2 3 4 5 Low High						
Time 1 2 3 4 5 Low High						
Resource Availability 1 2 3 4 5 Low High						

Key: In the boxes across the top, write the solution statements the team is considering. Rate each solution statement against the listed criteria by working across each row. The higher the total score, the greater the likelihood that the solution can be effectively implemented.

Criteria Rating Form for Problems

Criteria and Points	Weighted (if applicable)	Problem-Statement	Problem-Statement	Problem-Statement	Problem-Statement	Problem-Statement
Total Score						

Ranking Key: As a group identify and define the criteria to be used in evaluating problem statements. Enter the criteria and points (e.g., 1 = low, 5 = high in the boxes on the left. Write abbreviated problem statements in the boxes across the top. Work across, the form evaluating all problem statements against the first criterion, then the second, and so forth. As an option, you may decide to assign weighting factors to some criteria. If, for example, "release time" is critical, you may wish to weight it double the other factors, multiplying its score by 2 before entering it in the grid.

Criteria Rating Form for Solutions

Criteria and Points Weighted (if applicable)		Solution-Statement	Solution-Statement	Solution-Statement	Solution-Statement	Solution-Statement	Solution-Statement
Total Score							

Ranking Key: As a group identify and define the criteria to be used in evaluating potential solutions. Enter the criteria and points (e.g., 1 = low, 5 = high in the boxes on the left. Write abbreviated solution statements in the boxes across the top. Work across, the form evaluating all solution statements against the first criterion, then the second, and so forth. As an option, you may decide to assign weighting factors to some criteria. If, for example, "acceptability" is critical, you may wish to weight it double the other factors, multiplying its score by 2 before entering it in the grid.

Weighted Voting Form

Team Members	Option-Statement	Option-Statement	Option-Statement	Option-Statement	Option-Statement

Checksheet

ITEM	GROUP A	GROUP B	GROUP C	GROUP D	GROUP E	GROUP F	GROUP G